MW01165113

HITLER'S MEIN KAMPF

UNTIMELY MEDITATIONS

THE MIT PRESS
CAMBRIDGE, MASSACHUSETTS
LONDON, ENGLAND

ON HITLER'S MEIN KAMPF
THE POETICS OF NATIONAL SOCIALISM
ALBRECHT KOSCHORKE

TRANSLATED BY ERIK BUTLER

GOETHE INSTITUT

The translation of this work was supported by a grant from the Goethe-Institut which is funded by the German Ministry of Foreign Affairs.

This book was set in PF Din Text Pro by Toppan Best-set Premedia Limited. Printed and bound in the United States of America.

Library of Congress Cataloging-in-Publication Data
Names: Koschorke, Albrecht, 1958- author. | Butler, Erik, 1971- translator.
Title: On Hitler's Mein kampf : the poetics of National Socialism / Albrecht Koschorke ; translated by Erik Butler.
Other titles: Adolf Hitlers Mein Kampf. English
Description: Cambridge, MA : The MIT Press, 2017. | Series: Untimely meditations | Includes bibliographical references and index.
Identifiers: LCCN 2016028487 | ISBN 9780262533331 (pbk. : alk. paper)
Subjects: LCSH: Hitler, Adolf, 1889–1945. Mein Kampf. | Hitler, Adolf, 1889–1945--Philosophy. | National socialism--Philosophy. | National socialism--Psychological aspects. | Germany--Politics and government--20th century.
Classification: LCC DD247.H5 K66513 2017 | DDC 943.086092--dc23 LC record available at https://lccn.loc.gov/2016028487

10 9 8 7 6 5 4 3 2 1

CONTENTS

ON HITLER'S MEIN KAMPF

I

CRISIS SITUATIONS, PRECARIOUS MILIEUS,
LIMINAL ACTORS

1

Approaching the phenomenon of Adolf Hitler calls for broadening the scope of inquiry, not demonizing an individual. This measure is advisable if only because anyone can concoct a muddled combination of social critique and political mythology. Fortunately, very few manage to muster a powerful party in this way, much less win an entire people over to their cause. This sort of success can occur only under specific conditions. Analyzing these conditions—which is becoming more urgent in our own times of mounting radicalization—broaches the questions of how social myths (in the broadest sense) first emerge and what roles journalism and public discourse play in this process. How do the stories and histories that societies tell themselves about their past and their future arise? What images of collective being and self-diagnoses of conditions prevail in long-term social communication, both in everyday life and in public exchanges? How is it that certain ideas—especially ones that start out as marginal and circulate on a small scale—strike a chord with the population at large, and under what circumstances do they make the leap from the world of speeches and screeds into political action?

It has long been uncontroversial that social conditions are not simply "reflected" in their cultural representations. The connections between being and consciousness are many—and they are contested in many ways. One important reason is that instances of cultural symbolization constitute actions within their symbolic fields. They do not passively register given conditions in the manner of measuring devices; rather, and to varying degrees, they exercise transformative effects on them. In other words, it is not a "cold" and objective relationship between social facts and their cultural representation—between object and concept—so much as a "hot," circular dynamic.[1] Even by conventional logical standards, this implies an imbalance. By the same token, the semantic "heat of reaction" depends on the social energy expended. This energy takes shape in varied affective states anywhere along the spectrum of emotional investment extending from desire to hatred.

Stressing the performative quality of communication sheds light on the historical individuals, as well as authorities and institutions, that are responsible for ensuring that certain social self-representations achieve influence. It is scarcely possible to ascribe such a steering function only to the self-actualization of discourses. Their capacity to prevail depends on actors assuming positions within the cultural field. In order to propagate and achieve hegemonic validity, ideas rely on a substrate—along with whatever communicative infrastructure stands at the ready. Accordingly, inasmuch as the fabrication of social self-descriptions consists of creative acts—that is, performative actions on the part of individual or institutional agents—it is necessary to introduce a third dimension to the dichotomy between facts and ideas, social givens and cultural semantics. This function is exercised by parties who manage to lend form to an amorphous mass of facts, tendencies, and speculations and stamp them with a mode of description that finds recognition in ever-greater circles, until, finally, that mass becomes the "official" self-image of a society. It proves especially significant in phases of social upheaval, when a high degree of timeliness and topicality—evident in increasing readiness for violence—combines with an equally pronounced degree of inarticulacy, if not disorientation.

As a rule, states of social tension that lead to radical upheavals arise from an extremely complicated web of factors, which the people involved can comprehend only in part. In consequence, any account of the overall situation displays a high degree of arbitrariness, especially if meant to prove digestible in communicative terms and produce

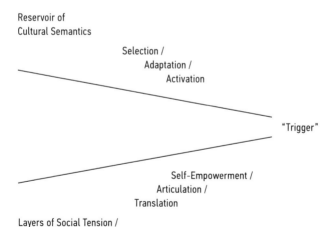

Reservoir of
Cultural Semantics

Selection /
Adaptation /
Activation

"Trigger"

Self-Empowerment /
Articulation /
Translation

Layers of Social Tension /
Collective State of Excitation

results on a broad scale. An effective description helps to articulate inarticulate experience by translating more or less diffuse emotional states—fear, hatred, feelings of belonging, desires, interests, and so on—into slogans and narratives that admit strong affective charges. In the process, it creates cognitive stabilization where none existed before, facilitating distinctions between friend and foe, "us" and "them." That is why a tertiary entity, which bridges collective agitation and a preexisting ideational edifice (or one adapted to the purposes at hand), often plays the role of a trigger, catalyzing a social explosion. Either the trigger points to a target for pent-up aggression, or it unites free-floating expectations, hopes, and desires to focus coordinated efforts of renewal. That said, these two strategies cannot be neatly separated from each other; they occur in hybrid forms without number.

Conventionally, the "trigger figure" is characterized as "the great man and the crowd." Political historiography from the times of Livy up to the revolutions of the twentieth century features exemplary individuals of this stripe, the leader of the angry masses. With due reverence, literature and opera—but especially history painting and film—have also provided the stage for such personages to take the spotlight. Sociology has done so, too. A model treatment is Gustave Le Bon's *The Crowd: A Study of the Popular Mind*. This work presents the leader as a man in the clutches of an obsessive idea, which he in turn manages to direct outward in order to hypnotize the masses.[2] For Le Bon, the crowd is purely passive and highly receptive to suggestion; only what appeals to its imitative instincts will work to guide it.

Contemporary sociology has found more sober explanations for "why," in the words of Michael Mann, "the masses do not revolt": they lack collective organization, and those in power command the logistics that sustained action would require.[3] All the same, the social psychology of old has the merit of being attentive to the force of ideas. To achieve power and hold it, controlling the lines of transportation and nodes of communication is not enough—even though doing so represents a necessary condition. In addition to technology and know-how, governing channels of communication over the long term requires an ideational vehicle—an ideology or more precisely a conglomerate of more or less coherent ideologemes conveying one's hegemonic claims far and wide. Interpretive sovereignty [*Deutungshoheit*] lies in the hands of whoever manages to combine a communicative system encompassing the realm to be ruled with a semantic order that succeeds in achieving universal dimensions.

The preceding affords a more precise picture of the function filled by the trigger and mouthpiece. This figure works on two levels. First, in "organizational" terms (Mann), he brings together collective stirrings on a modest scale—say, local revolts—and feeds the impulses they embody into an efficient communicative network. This may involve communication among elites or the educated, trade channels and the flow of commodities, and/or underground organizations or subcultures. Second, the trigger sets an igniting idea to the powder keg of social upheaval. Only when a suitable relay between collective energies and cultural semantics has been switched on, through a kind of fuse, can deep-reaching social transformation be set in motion. The question is where to find the igniting idea. Le Bon drew a complex picture of ideogenesis. On the example of socialism, he demonstrated that ideologies have a long incubation period. As they spread, they can not only transfer down from the elevated classes to the masses but also drift upward in the social hierarchy. In his eyes, the latter case merits special consideration:

> This reaction of the lower upon the higher social classes is the more curious, owing to the circumstance that the beliefs of the crowd always have their origin to a greater or less extent in some higher idea, which has often remained without influence in the sphere in which it was evolved. Leaders and agitators, subjugated by this higher idea, take hold of it, distort it and create a sect which distorts it afresh, and then propagates it amongst the masses, who carry the process of deformation still further. Become a popular truth the idea returns, as it were, to its source and exerts an influence on the upper classes of a nation. In the long run it is intelligence that shapes the destiny of the world, but very indirectly.[4]

Ideologies, according to Le Bon's account, spread in circles. At the outset, they are more or less esoteric and hold few social consequences. They achieve explosive force when a certain, obsessive personality type takes them on and declares them the mission of a sectarian movement. Now, they progressively enter into more, and more expansive, communicative networks. Under favorable circumstances, they manage to infiltrate the affective realm and interests of broader circles, overcome sectarian limitations, and assume increasingly pronounced popular traits. By way of this circuitous route, ultimately they come again to exercise influence on the educated classes. Nor does the ideational substrate remain unaffected by all these transfers. At several points, Le Bon mentions a mechanism of distortion. As a result, the message, when it comes to bear historical weight, may have but little to do with the intentions that motivated its inaugurator.

2

After it is extracted from the dichotomy of masses and leader that prevailed during the years around 1900, Le Bon's phase model proves heuristically useful in a larger framework. With certain modifications, it applies to many ideological movements. We can devise a typology of social catalysts that take up available intellectual material, deform it along sectarian lines (that is, radicalize it in most cases), and then bring it into circulation to marked effect. In particular, two professional groups, or milieus, are at work. To a great extent, the one flows into the other, but they also fulfill separately discernible functions. The first comprises preachers, reformist civil servants, physicians, and other educated parties with an income. Their emblematic figure is the educator of the people, motivated by a worldview. This group plays a significant role in the history of nationalism (for instance, in nineteenth-century France)[5] up to the various ethnonationalisms of the twentieth century (such as in postcolonial Africa). The second group has a less secure livelihood. It typically includes freelance journalists, writers, artists, bohemians, intellectuals who are unemployed or work irregularly, and dropouts from the educational system or other state institutions. Their emblematic figure is the political pamphleteer. This milieu can be summed up by the term *precariat*—provided the word is taken to refer not to those permanently hung out to dry but to the social mode of operation prevailing in tenuous or potential elites. The members of this milieu are waiting in hope that their historical day will arrive. In general, the grandiosity of their plans for changing the world stands in inverse proportion to the chance of ever realizing them—unless exceptional circumstances come to their aid.

A classic study of this kind of precariat—long before the term became fashionable—was written by the historian Robert Darnton. In *The Literary Underground of the Old Regime*, he presents a generational conflict within the French Enlightenment. Although the grand *philosophes* like Voltaire and Jean Le Rond d'Alembert successfully struggled for and achieved access to Parisian high society and were supported by the regime through pensions and patronage, younger people who flocked to Paris after the 1770s could find no livelihood even approximately commensurate with their worth. They gathered in the literary underground and "survived by doing the dirty work of society—spying for the police and peddling pornography."[6] Their wretched existence as "versifiers," "would-be authors," and "famished scribblers"[7] filled them with a twofold resentment—against the regime, which had no use for them, and against the literary-philosophical establishment, where they desired a position. As Darnton puts it:

> the top of Paris, the *tout Paris,* had little room for ambitious young men on the make, perhaps because, as sociologists claim, rising status groups tend to become exclusive; perhaps because France suffered from a common ailment of developing countries: a surplus population of overeducated and underemployed *littérateurs* and lawyers.[8]

These are the people—unsettled minds such as Jean-Paul Marat (and many others)—who wrote embittered pamphlets and, in so doing, provided something like the intellectual ferment for the revolution in France. Torn between the cynicism of the disadvantaged and moralizing outrage, between despair and megalomania, they made the liberal and egalitarian principles of Jean-Jacques Rousseau's generation their own—except that, in contrast to the older generation of the Enlightenment, they lacked the security of a state pension. At night, they earned their meager livelihood as pornographers, but during the day they lent their hatred ever cruder expression in screeds. "It was from such visceral hatred," Darnton writes, "not from the refined abstractions of the contented cultural elite, that the extreme Jacobin revolution found its authentic voice."[9]

Insofar as these findings admit generalization and bear on the trigger typology proposed here, radical social changes are catalyzed only indirectly by inaugurators of new social visions who hold academic positions or otherwise enjoy a privileged situation. The key role falls to an intellectual precariat that takes up these ideas, disseminates them—initially through subcultural channels—and thereby, under the pressure of its own beggary, radicalizes them. In the passage quoted above, Darnton lists the sociological conditions that favor such a trigger function—a surplus of young men (underemployed academics, half-educated or self-taught parties) whose upward ambitions are blocked by predecessors whom they perceive as self-satisfied and corrupt. These circumstances call to mind violence-prone milieus in developing countries today, such as those of militant Islam. That said, this social profile would not be complete without young idealists from privileged backgrounds who are deeply dissatisfied with societal conditions, make themselves advocates of the disenfranchised, and join the precariat of their own free will, as it were.

Time and again and for varying reasons, history has witnessed the rise of "precarious generations." At such times, a marked number of trailblazers, radical journalists, politically erratic aesthetes, heterodox theologians, and people who are uprooted or occupy insecure positions set the tone. Such crisis generations have played a key role in the success of nationalism, which is certainly the most powerful European ideology of the last two hundred years. The history of nationalism offers a touchstone for Le Bon's phase model. On German soil, its literary beginnings reach back to the so-called Anacreontic school—that is, to the circle around Johann Wilhelm Ludwig Gleim. Employed as secretary of the cathedral chapter at Halberstadt and otherwise more inclined to convivial songs about wine and women—which have left traces in the second verse of the

Deutschlandlied[10]—Gleim managed to tap into a new market for poetry with his *Preußische Kriegslieder*, which he composed during the Seven Years' War. All in all, however, his work amounts to little more than a "poetic exaltation of absolutist cabinet wars" fought by mercenary armies thrown together from regional confraternities.[11] Here, Prussian patriotism still constituted a poetic experiment. Similar traits are displayed by the "folkloric rediscovery of 'the people'" in other European lands around 1800. As Eric J. Hobsbawm has written, it "provided the foundation for many a subsequent nationalist movement" but was "in no sense ... yet a political movement of the people concerned, nor did it imply any political ... programme." Hobsbawm views the reinterpretation of folklore in terms of national tradition as "the work of enthusiasts" belonging to an elite that, often enough, was not even autochthonous. Only later did a new "body of activists" seize the "national idea," and it took even longer for the masses to demonstrate enthusiasm for it.[12]

The founding of a nation follows a peculiar logic, because as Ulrich Bielefeld has put it, such unity must first summon forth its "political correlative"—the "actual, empirical people."[13] Doing so poses a challenge in terms of ideology and popular pedagogy, but it also offers intellectuals—who have the task of effecting transfers between standing conditions and ideas—considerable, if informal, possibilities for exercising influence:

> To paraphrase Max Weber, parties interested in culture recognize an opportunity here. Now, political

intellectuals emerge. No longer are they just advisers, administrators, priests, and mandarins; even if they do not occupy the summit of power themselves, they receive an assignment that reaches far beyond offering counsel to potentates and performing administrative tasks. In varied form—be it in terms of literature, history, science, or ideology (in addition to politics and organization)—they set to work explaining the whole, the essence of the nation, culture, and society, thereby fashioning its image.[14]

In this undertaking, the two groups named above play a key role, albeit in different ways. Some (civil servants and teachers) implement the national project administratively and didactically—usually operating in the framework of existing institutions. Meanwhile, others (political intellectuals, who belong more to the precariat, whether by necessity or choice, though they harbor elite aspirations) exploit the temporal delay between the national idea and its fulfillment in order to elaborate their activist and revolutionary programs. Given its high-flown, utopian nature, the political project of exalting the nation—which is often nothing more than the artificial product of historical mythology—exerts an irresistible charm on the precarious intellectual. Accordingly, this is the site of intersections between politics and aesthetics, forays drifting between ideology and art. Nationalism has long provided a main source for the topos of the statesman-as-artist that his loyal adherents celebrate. One quotation will suffice to attest as much. It comes from a man with a humble background who felt stigmatized because of a physical defect. Despite unfavorable circumstances, he managed to obtain a doctorate in literature, dabbled in poetry with echoes of late Expressionism, and finally became the chief propagandist of a terrorist regime. Joseph Goebbels has the floor:

> Forming the masses into a nation, and a nation into a state—that has always been the deepest goal of true politics. ... The statesman is also an artist. For him the nation is exactly what the stone is for the sculptor. *Führer* and masses, that is as little of a problem as, say, painter and color.[15]

3

Ideological dynamics of this kind occur in a wide array of ethnonationalist contexts, which demands a comparative perspective, such as Jacques Sémelin provides in *Purify and Destroy: The Political Uses of Massacre and Genocide*. The author notes a shared feature of the movements with regard to "ideological genesis":

> In the lead-up to the committing of a violent act as such, we can observe that its framework of meaning will have invariably been constructed by "intellectuals" who, ostensibly working for the "good" of their country, have articulated radical analyses of its situation. These analyses more often than not lead in practice to the stigmatisation of a particular group. ... The term "intellectual" is perhaps not always the most appropriate one

to use. ... It would probably be more accurate to refer to them as "identity entrepreneurs." ...

Whatever the scenario, these intellectuals for the most part belong to professions of the mind. ... Teachers or professors, they have studied at university, sometimes without completing the academic course (and so perhaps harbouring feelings of failure). They are journalists, academics, doctors or engineers; or they could be artists or men of the church. In the crisis situation their country is undergoing, and faced with frustrations that they themselves feel personally, it is often they who will first start formulating a "solution" to resolve these problems, a solution that they will doggedly defend using the strength of their pen or their discourse.[16]

Sémelin lists the examples—the ideological essayist Alfred Rosenberg, the nationalist writer Dobrica Ćosić (who played an important role laying the groundwork for Slobodan Milošević), and the militant seminarian, journalist, and ultimately president Grégoire Kayibanda (who was one of the ideological precursors to paving the way to genocide in Rwanda). Any one of these figures, taken alone, would seem to offer abundant proof for the observation of a Rwandan survivor that learning "does not make man better, it makes him more efficient."[17] Many violent regimes of the twentieth century formed under similar circumstances. Their guiding idea of an organically unified ethnic nation [Staatsvolk] generally demanded victims in proportion to the disunity of their actual conditions. A corresponding level of political-mythological fantasy is required to infuse a national spirit into an artificial state—which, often enough, emerges between the arbitrary borders left behind by colonial schemes.[18] Tellingly, most modern dictators have come from the conspiratorial milieu where bohemia, criminality, and ideological radicalism fuse into an impenetrable amalgam; at any rate, they tend to have entertained contacts with it in early years.[19]

In this context, another feature of these triggering figures comes into view. It is best designated by the key word *liminality*. Victor Turner coined the term to refer to the threshold status that groups or individuals enter when a crisis situation prevails. The temporary dissolution of status positions, hierarchies, and social structures is matched by the mental state of those experiencing events. Psychically, they are pushed beyond normal borders, moving into zones where visionary perspectives and delusions no longer admit strict divisions, and stand closer both to the realm of the sacred and to madness than ordinary circumstances allow.

Such characteristics hold for the parties being discussed here. Le Bon writes that leader personalities who are capable of hypnotizing the masses because they themselves stand under the spell of a great idea "are especially recruited from the ranks of ... morbidly nervous, excitable, half-deranged persons ... bordering on madness."[20] The same might be said of many founders or renewers of countries that are facing states of political exception. In many ways, they have a liminal mode of being—in the first place, as a result of the heightened collective excitement that social upheaval entails; second, through the fluctuations of their own lives in terms of material security, status, and group belonging; finally, through a personal disposition that fits the social situation, as it were. This includes the quest for a heightened experience of community and euphoric fraternization—as well as the individual inclination toward social visions that are more or less arbitrarily constituted and, under certain conditions, achieve delusional dimensions. When Turner describes the liminal state as "a realm of pure possibility whence novel configurations of ideas and relations may arise," and how it yields a world of "as-if,"[21] he makes it clear that this condition involves an undirected "fever of ideas" among its actors, which shoots far beyond social norms.

Many great historical innovations have derived from individuals who were borderline cases in their contemporaries' eyes—who counted as monomaniacs and troublemakers, if not as outright crackpots. Because most people of this stripe achieve nothing and their effects remain limited to inconsequential pronouncements, they usually pass unnoticed. However, under certain circumstances, fertile ground develops for their ideas, which then, after the fact, seem to have been visionary or prophetic. As we have noted, in addition to the sphere of religion, the history of (ethno)nationalism in Europe and elsewhere is marked by figures whose apparition, in calm retrospect, bears the signs of a certain craziness. In the context of Prussian-German nationalism, key figures from the period of the Anti-Napoleonic Wars of Liberation (such as the legendary father of gymnastics and patriotic activist Friedrich Ludwig Jahn) display these traits. In addition to poets of middling stature such as Theodor Körner, their circle includes a highly talented author who wandered from one front to another as he grew increasingly fanatical in his nationalist hatred for Napoleon—Heinrich von Kleist.

The twentieth century abounds in such figures, too—even if one disregards those who paved the way for or led totalitarian movements. They include, for example, Ettore Tolomei, the Italian geographer and linguist who, from 1901 on, Italianized all the German place names in South Tirol with a singular disregard for linguistic accuracy. Although the project started out as little more than an obsessive private enterprise, after the First World War—when South Tirol fell under Italian sovereignty—the list that he devised provided the official basis for the politics of nomenclature in the region. Tolomei's crude translations and false etymologies offer an enduring record of the amalgamated fantasy and violence through which projects of nationalization are implemented.

Especially given the challenges faced by developing countries in the postcolonial or postimperial age, even seemingly incoherent ideologies can prove relatively functional. The need to "reinvent autochthonous identities" in young African or central Asian states can hardly avoid the genre of political fantasy. This holds for the slogan of *Ivorité* promulgated by Henri Konan Bédié, the erstwhile president of the Ivory Coast, which led to a civil war. It applies to the violent autochthonization of Uzbekistan on the part of Islam Karimov, who has wielded dictatorial powers since 1991.[22] The former president of Turkmenistan, Saparmurat

Niyazov, is an especially bizarre case. His book *Ruhnama, or Book of the Soul*—a conglomeration of historical myths, political doctrine, and many other ingredients—invokes the ancient venerability of the Turkmen ethnic nation.[23] This work, which appeared in two volumes in 2001 and 2004 and was made compulsory reading throughout the land, may be the last cult book of modern dictatorship in the tradition of Hitler's *Mein Kampf*.

The figures above do not all qualify as triggers in the same measure. Typological generalizations are always flawed: they provide an overview but fail to account for the particulars of individual cases. Still, it may be that social upheaval regularly gives rise to combustible sociotopes where the "heat of reaction" enables ruthless breaks with standing institutions and received ideas. When such radicalization yields lasting results, its agents can portray them as having been part of a greater plan all along. But while events are occurring, radicalization displays semantic excess: periods lacking orientation are characterized by free and loose efforts to fabricate meaning. Even for people who will later support a movement, the pronouncements and writings that crisis situations bring forth soon prove difficult to appreciate. Usually, the consequence is a very selective—and altogether tortuous—canonization of the movement's pioneering ideological words and deeds.[24] Sober assessment from a distance often discerns ridiculous features that were not evident at the time.

That said, a greater proximity exists between laughable events and dreadful ones than calmer ages would like to admit. Just because a position seems merely dubious from the vantage point of argumentative superiority doesn't make it any less dangerous. Moreover, the social margins do not produce only extremist views. There are many channels connecting liminal regions with the everyday world; the border between these spheres is porous and shifting. Even social conditions that appear ordinary and self-evident harbor mad schemes that have been forgotten and, as it were, deactivated. Accordingly, one should bear in mind just how fragile equilibrium is. The abnormal and even the delusional are not cut from a different cloth than what counts as normal. Instead—and as terrible as it sounds—it just seems that way because they prove so fateful under conditions of extreme social tension.

II

HITLER'S *MEIN KAMPF*: IDEOLOGY AND DECISION

1

One feature that modern dictatorships share is the prominent role they assign to an aging medium—the book. From this perspective, book culture found its last, hypertrophic form in the totalitarianism of the twentieth century. As documented in the anthology *Despoten dichten*,[1] many dictators had literary ambitions, and some of them based their violent reigns on a veritable cult of the book. As much as the works of Hitler, Stalin, Mao, and Gadhafi differ in terms of style and ideology, the regimes share a bibliocentric orientation. To simplify matters to their ideal and type, one may speak of the book as the symbolic center of totalitarian systems. In each case, it constitutes the sacral core of state propaganda, which otherwise employs more modern media—radio, film, and television. Distributed among party officials and even to the entire population, the book possesses the character of a constitution. At any rate, it is endowed with authority that receives due honor in the regime's public displays and networks of power. The guiding idea is to lay an enduring foundation for a political structure that, having emerged from the confusion of war and revolution, proves highly precarious in terms of legitimacy and stability. As such, the situation to which the book reacts is liminal to a large extent. Its inhabitants are precisely those actors whose operations and influences are described in the first part of this essay. As an ideological groundwork—whether ethnonationalist or socialist (whereby elements of both are often combined)—the book fulfills a quasi-religious function and is meant to assume the legacy of the holy works of the great world religions. This accounts for the tension between the propagandistic use of technological and industrial media, on the one hand, and, on the other, the archaizing rituals conducted around the sacred book—where bibliophilic pomp, fetishism, talismanic contact, and other kinds of magical staging merge into a distinct syndrome. We have noted what may be the final example of the genre—the *Ruhnama, or Book of the Soul* by Saparmurat Niyazov, published in 2001. This book is meant to establish the national identity of the Turkmen people. It was read during television broadcasts and on official occasions. For years, it provided the sole reading material at schools and universities. Indeed, an oversized memorial was erected for the book in the capital. There is even a copy floating around the earth in a space capsule.[2]

All of these dictatorial books play a central role in cleansing operations that break with the past and, at the same time, reinvent it to self-aggrandizing ends. These works counter the confusion of the present, which seems to offer no stay, with a rigorous—and ultimately terroristic— will to order. A combative aversion to the tumult detected everywhere is inscribed in them and constitutes their driving force. To understand their authors' motivations, it is important to recognize that terror and catharsis, fear and purification, do not occur only in ancient tragedies; they also play a role in modern ideologies of power. This fact holds in spite of the familiar irony that dictators usually increase the very chaos they pretend to oppose—only to fall victim, in the end, to the spiraling disorder they have whipped on to even greater fury.

How does the dictatorial book establish order? Ultimately, this is a question of how ideology functions in general. It is necessary to distinguish content and gesture, on the one hand, and between the various circles to which totalitarian writing is addressed, on the other. The holy writ of dictators claims to offer adherents a meaningful orientation. At the same time, closer semantic analysis reveals such writing to be inconsistent and eclectic in the highest degree. Other factors must be considered to explain the effects of these works, then. They include their ritual status—which, as is often the case for religious writings, is meant to make their contents immune to criticism (which would strip away their magic). Moreover, the particular conditions governing encounters with the book itself must be taken into account. Very few people ever read it in its entirety, if they read it at all; others know only excerpts or quotations that have entered into general circulation. As a result, numerous concentric rings of initiation emerge— degrees in a political priesthood, whose representatives enjoy varying levels of distinction among the vast mass of nonreaders and play the part of their mentors. Although modern propaganda, in principle, is addressed to all at once, attendant conditions give rise to a system of partial symbolic participation based on the book, which comprises manifold gradations corresponding to various levels of distinction. This helps explain why the confusion that these cultic books exhibit does not undermine their authority. If anything, the opposite is the case: the greater the obscurity and ambiguity of their phraseology, the easier it is to employ their contents selectively. As a result, the interest groups that heed the "call" obtain greater internal leeway. Significance of a corresponding magnitude marks the dictatorial text's gestural signals, which are not directed toward the uninitiated so much as the elect circle of potential elites within the new regime.

2

Having offered these preliminary considerations, our attention now turns to the first dictatorial book of the twentieth century—Adolf Hitler's programmatic *Mein Kampf*. In contrast to later examples of the genre, this work's effect has survived the collapse of the regime it helped to found. Its remarkably divided reception merits notice. Officially, *Mein Kampf* could not be reprinted in Germany until the end of 2015. The Bavarian Ministry of Finance—which unwillingly holds copyright due to a series of chance events—had restricted its availability by juridical means. Vehement public debate attended the publication of the edition overseen by the Munich Institute for Contemporary History, which includes scholarly commentary meant to neutralize the danger of ideological contamination as a kind of *cordon sanitaire*.[3] That said, it was not difficult, even before the prohibition on reprinting had expired, to gain access to the original in used bookstores or online. Outside Germany, the book has long sold well and on a broad scale. In Turkey, Egypt, India, and other countries, it has been reprinted time and again and "moved" in considerable quantities. At the same time, academic readers—if they even bother to subject themselves to what Hitler cooked up—uniformly note how boring, unoriginal, jargon-laden, stylistically butchered, embarrassingly rabid, and altogether ludicrous they find the text. Reaction of this kind already occurred in the 1920s; fatefully, it inspired confidence that the author had no future in politics.[4] It is all the more puzzling, then, that this text was ever able to achieve resonance on a significant scale, much less cast its spell on readers today (or why legal and editorial measures of caution are taken all the same).

What is the core fascination exercised by Hitler's broadsheet, which produced such disastrous effects? Whom does the book address, and why? All in all, discussions either endorse or reject the views presented.[5] Readers praise Hitler's vigorously authentic style or fault him for giving himself the airs of a great author while scribbling out incoherent fantasies of hatred in a state of exalted intellectual amateurism. To achieve greater psychological depth and focus, then, an analysis of the text and the signals it broadcasts is in order. *Mein Kampf* cannot simply be boiled down to an ideological message directed to all readers; nor should a homogeneous audience be assumed. What divergent expectations does the book anticipate? What methods of inclusion does Hitler employ when he performs his propagandistic thrust: whom does he "take along," and who is "not admitted"? What enticements does he extend, what kind of attention does he awaken, and what desires does all this satisfy?

3

One approach to these questions lies in the narrative structure of the first part of *Mein Kampf*. In a key passage, Hitler discusses his relationship to the Social Democrats. In keeping with the scheme of the book—which, like a political *Bildungsroman*, aligns the evolution of National Socialist ideology with a (largely fictionalized) story of personal development—the confrontation with Social Democracy is embedded in an episode from the author's "Years of Study and Suffering in Vienna." Hitler claims that he was working as an unskilled laborer in construction. Pressured by union agitators, he got caught up in heated discussions—until his adversaries threatened physical violence and drove him away from the site. This experience, according to Hitler, underlies his hatred for—still more, his disgust with—Social Democrats, who "mislead" or "seduce" workers.[6]

The tone shifts just as soon as Hitler touches on this theme. Up to this point, his description of the miseries of the Viennese underclasses demonstrates relative sensitivity and compassion; on this basis, he elaborates a series of sociopolitical demands. Now, however, the style changes, and paranoid denunciations erupt. Hitler speaks of the "monstrous work of poisoning" pursued by the Red press[7] and how the *Volk*, which has been led astray, must be protected from it. He affirms that it spews forth a "veritable barrage of lies and slanders" against political opponents. In response, he advocates "combating poison gas with poison gas."[8] An emphatic passage reads, "Terror at the place of employment, in the factory, in the meeting hall and on the occasion of demonstrations will always be successful unless opposed by equal terror."[9]

Whoever enters into an "autobiographical pact"[10] with the author and reads *Mein Kampf* as an account of his life's political journey is immediately struck by the asymmetry of the provocation (a political dispute at a construction site) and the ensuing reaction (a fantasy of poison gas). All the same, we can surmise why, at precisely this juncture, Hitler works himself up into his first, hateful tirade. For one, he must conceal an autobiographical fabrication. As Brigitte Hamann has convincingly demonstrated in *Hitler's Vienna: A Dictator's Apprenticeship*, no evidence exists that the young Hitler—scrawny and awkward as he was— ever performed hard physical labor.[11] The story about coercion by unions on the scaffolding is a cock-and-bull story borrowed from the right-wing, nationalist press. Hitler acquired all that he knew about Social Democracy by feverishly reading newspapers and brochures. His political struggles during this period—if he had any at all—were limited to agitated monologues in the men's shelter.[12]

Another reason for Hitler's hatred of Social Democracy is political in nature. Recalling the hardship of the Viennese period, Hitler thanks good fortune for "hurling me, despite all resistance, into a world of misery and poverty, this making me acquainted with those for whom I was later to fight."[13] Social problems, he writes, cannot be solved by condescending acts of charity. Instead, it is a matter of taking on, and from the ground up, "basic deficiencies in the organization of our economic and cultural life."[14] His demands—starting with the improvement of living conditions and educational institutions—agree with many contemporary initiatives for social reform. To this extent, the programs that Hitler proposes and those of the hated Social Democrats share a number of points in common. As regards techniques for leading the masses, there are passages that mirror his opponents' methods—just in a different key, as it were. These crowds, Hitler tellingly writes, are like "the woman" [*dem Weibe*] who, because she "would rather bow to a strong man than dominate a weakling," fails to perceive the "shameless spiritual terrorization" that her conduct entails.[15] Of course, the "brutality" of intolerant doctrineering—that is, the same charge he levels at the Social Democrats—would become his own precept and standard.

All the while, Hitler—the son of a civil servant who had risen socially and joined the bourgeoisie—presents a picture of the lower classes that is deeply divided. As an amorphous, blind "mass," they earn his hatred and scorn. As the *Volk*, they are idealized. This is precisely what sets Hitler's view apart from the Social Democratic party platform. In contrast to the Marxian concept of class, the key term for Hitler is *Volk*, which he conceived of as an ethnic and national unit from the very beginning. Two fundamentally divergent assessments of political conflict follow from this difference. Division along the lines of class sees social struggles occurring between the top and the bottom. This entails an internationalist orientation: the Workers' International faces the International of Capital. Whereas with this model, the line of social division is horizontal, the nationalist perspective—especially in the extremist, biologistic form that Hitler advocates—sees a vertical principle of separation at work. Viewed in national terms, all members of a people are related in essence. Inner division, then, amounts to a betrayal of their shared nature. By the same token, members of other peoples remain fundamentally alien. Connivance with them amounts to betrayal, too—betrayal of loyalty to one's own nation.

Juxtaposed in this schematic fashion, socialism and nationalism stand as two incompatible models for inclusion and exclusion. Deciding between them means sacrificing part of the political potential available. Either one opts for an ethnic program—which, in a multiethnic state like Austria, splinters into any number of oppositions and (failing to acknowledge the preeminence of the social question) misses the chance to achieve broad popular support—or, alternately, one follows a social agenda that misses the opportunities afforded by betting on the card of nationality. The Austrian political landscape presented Hitler with possibilities for both these models in the form of the All-German and the Christian-Social parties.[16]

The program that Hitler envisioned for the National Socialist German Workers Party (NSDAP) wagered that both promises—the national agenda and the social one—could be fulfilled in the same breath. In terms of the electorate, this meant appealing both to the nationalistically inclined petty bourgeoisie, with its protectionist and xenophobic reflexes, and to workers, who listened to slogans of class struggle. Sociologically, it corresponded precisely to Hitler's own development as the scion of a petty bourgeois family that had ascended in rank. It also matches the posture he affects in *Mein Kampf*, where he pretends to have shared the fate of the simple people in his years of hardship and poverty (while at the same time carefully keeping his distance from them). This fabrication—to once have belonged to the army of laborers and, simultaneously, to have achieved unique insights into overarching political conditions by way of intensive study—destines him to become the mentor, indeed the guardian, of the working classes. The role of *Führer*, which combines the communitarian pathos of populism with authoritarian contempt for the crowd, is already in evidence.

As Hannah Arendt puts it, Hitler's program "offered a synthesis supposed to lead to national unity, a semantic solution whose double trademark of 'German' and 'Worker' connected the nationalism of the right with the internationalism of the left"; thereby, it "stole the political contents of the other parties."[17] The matter bears on Social Democracy, in particular: rather than set the antagonist at the opposite end of the political spectrum, Hitler's ideological maneuvering made his rival occupy the same terrain.[18] The problem does not involve points of contradiction so much as— propagandistically disadvantageous—areas of political overlap in the concerns shared by Social Democracy and National Socialism.

So how did Hitler set about establishing the ideological distinction he deemed necessary? The narrative design of *Mein Kampf* provides the answer. Immediately following his discussion of the social question, Hitler elaborates his anti-Semitic conspiracy theory. The struggle to be the masses' spokesman amounts to combat at extremely close quarters. Everything depends on tearing the masses away from socialist agitators and shaping them according to *völkisch* principles. When rivalry is this close, demonization proves indispensable. The hobgoblin that Hitler evokes is whoever does not conform to the scheme of "the national." For racists and partisans of the *Volk* at the turn of the century, whose writings he drew on when fashioning his eclectic worldview, this party is the Jew. (Largely for tactical reasons, other enemies—such as Catholics, who were loyal to Rome and therefore might count as anti-German—do not enter the picture.)[19]

In keeping with his maxim that the public's objections must be rebutted preemptively,[20] Hitler presents his "transformation into an anti-Semite" as the result of an arduous inner struggle—practically a religious conversion.[21] Only with great effort, he lets it be known, did he overcome his original tolerance in matters of religion—which formerly had prompted him to take offense at anti-Jewish campaigns in the press. Time and again, he admits, he suffered "relapses."[22] But now that the battle against toleration, humanitarian considerations, and good taste is over, Jewish world conspiracy offers a phantasm that smooths over any and all gaps in his line of argument. By identifying Marxism as the central element in this plot, Hitler can declare himself the savior of the German *Volk* and proceed to annex the people to his worldview: "Only a knowledge of the Jews provides the key with which to comprehend the inner, and consequently real, aims of Social Democracy."[23]

This conspiracy theory is as difficult to attack as any other. To outsiders, it seems so thoroughly murky as not to warrant serious engagement. What is more, it possesses a built-in mechanism that makes it resistant to disproof: anyone seeking to refute it may be accused of having already fallen for the ruses of the Jewish press, thereby proving the theory's accuracy. In this manner, the theory seals itself off from the outside and achieves inner coherence. For the movement's followers, its attractiveness lies in precisely this closedness, which ensures a strong group identity internally and projects a figure of the enemy externally. From the leader's standpoint, the call to counter the conspiracy represents a conditional offer of love that weaves together promises and threats: follow me, and let yourselves be molded into a people according to my vision so I won't be forced to despise and destroy you.[24]

Having accounted for his "transformation into an anti-Semite"—supposedly at a construction site in Vienna—Hitler lays the groundwork for his belated working through of the trauma of 1918. In chapter 7 of part I of *Mein Kampf*, he tells how he temporarily fell blind in a poison gas attack and had to be hospitalized. Right after this episode, one reads: "For a long time there had already been something indefinite but repulsive in the air."[25] Now, however, the matter at issue is no longer gas warfare but rather—by way of a metonymic bridge—revolutionary activities at home. The real catastrophe that caught the warrior for the fatherland off-guard is capitulation: "And then one day, suddenly and unexpectedly, the calamity descended."[26] Hitler salvages his image of the German people by blaming the revolution on "a few Jewish youths."[27] He presents the kaiser as having been cheated by the "leaders of Marxism."[28] Even though he acknowledges the former's weakness, he leaves his authority intact. In denial, all available energy is redirected toward the real, inner enemy: "There is no making pacts with Jews; there can only be the hard: either—or."[29]

4

A legend surrounds Hitler's bellicose work, which has been served up time and again: in spite of its massive distribution to schools and libraries and despite the fact that it was handed out as a matter of duty at civil registries, the book is supposed to have remained unread because, all in all, it is unreadable.[30] The legend warrants notice insofar as Hitler, in the preface, does not address himself to "strangers, but to those adherents of the movement who belong to it with their hearts."[31] Five hundred pages later, in the second volume, he bluntly declares that "the mass of people is lazy," never reads books, and has only a brief attention span, anyway.[32] Any readers who have stuck with him until this point may therefore consider themselves to number among the initiated—whose understanding comes at the expense of others. This fits with Hannah Arendt's observation that totalitarian regimes are organized on the model of secret societies and operate according to a system distinguished by subtle gradations of participation.[33] That said, the rub of the National Socialist ideology is that it openly displayed—to anyone with eyes to see—not just its popular [*völkisch*] and spectacular aspect but also, and to an astonishing degree, the arcana of its techniques of power.

Indeed, Hitler candidly discusses how to employ the tools of propaganda. This fact manifestly contradicts the widespread assumption that ideologies function only if they conceal the ways and means that they are fabricated. *Mein Kampf* is arranged so that one may read it on two levels. For pages on end, it holds forth about Marxist intrigue and Jewish freeloading. Thereby, it satisfies the same primitive, ideological hunger of readers who, a few years after the book's publication, would feed on Julius Streicher's news-paper, *Der Stürmer*. In this capacity, *Mein Kampf* stands as a testimony to blind racial mania.[34] But for all that, Hitler does not present himself as a fanatical Jew hater from the outset. Instead, he makes a point of authenticating his anti-Semitism by depicting it as the result of a learning process. On this score, his account agrees with historical research, even if he backdates his "transformation." No anti-Semitic remarks are recorded from his time in Vienna. He struck this tone only when declaiming in Munich beer halls—in other words, after his decision (dating to the "years of upheaval, in 1918–19")[35] to "go into politics."[36]

Why does Hitler—who is so fond of declaring that even his earliest decisions were "unwavering" and who constantly undermines the principle of development inherent in auto-biography by affirming that he has never changed any of his fundamental positions—why does Hitler not claim always to have held a "rock-solid" and "steadfast" opinion about world Jewry? One reason, as suggested above, is that he thought it more effective, in psychological terms, to meet readers on the level of whatever human compassion they still felt, instead of foisting a completed dogma on them.[37] In the early stages of radical political movements, it is still necessary to consider skepticism on the part of those who have not yet been fully converted. However, the strategic placement of the conversion narrative points to a second aspect of the book concerned less with ideology itself than with its technical production.

At this juncture, a remark on the circumstances attending the genesis of *Mein Kampf* is in order. Even though it has long been rumored that parties close to Hitler contributed to the book's writing, the greatest part was authored by Hitler himself, on his own.[38] All the same—and counter to what the book itself claims—*Mein Kampf* is not the result of the individual's power of creation. For one, the typescript was reworked on the way to press. Tellingly—and to the detriment of style—the changes introduced elements of speech into the written document.[39] Nor is everything that the inmate at Landsberg Prison typed out early in the morning fashioned entirely from scratch. Hitler recorded what had proven successful in *völkisch* circles. Indeed, he did not even shape his own profile as a propagandist. Rather, he owed this image to the influence, support, and training provided by the Bavarian Reichswehr, which employed him as a contractor immediately after the war.[40] Naturally, Hitler has to deny that his ideological fanaticism followed from personal opportunism. But *Mein Kampf* does not deny the strategic nature of the ideology of which the author has made himself the spokesman. In consequence, Hitler's look back at his years in Vienna serves two wholly different purposes. On the one hand, it is meant to obscure his much later—and much less ideologically commendable—calling as a political agitator. On the other hand, it tells political followers and allies, almost in textbook fashion, how to craft language suited for the masses: sharpen it to a single point and hold fast—"unwaveringly," "with an iron will," and so on.

Mein Kampf is constructed in such a way that confrontation with the Social Democrats and discussion of the "Jewish question" relate to each other as problem and solution. The treatment of the theme yields a kind of two-story structure. On the level of ideology, the essential message is that the eradication of Jewry—which is supposed to constitute the driving force behind capital and anticapitalism alike (conspiracy theories are confusing to the uninitiated)— will end class struggle as such. But in terms of party tactics, another aspect occupies the foreground—the demonization of political rivals who, in advancing partially similar socio-political measures, also claim to represent the masses. The narrative design of *Mein Kampf* is absolutely plain in this regard—and it is likely that the fact did not escape readers who were schooled in politics. On this level, attention does not fall on the *what* of ideology so much as the *how* of working it to propagandistic ends.

5

Evidence abounds that Hitler sought, above all, to address followers who were interested in the way that power is constituted [*Machart von Macht*]. For the narrower circle of his adherents, *Mein Kampf* provided a manual—which is also how such parties understood the book.[41] Indeed, the very choice of this medium implies a practical orientation: Hitler thought that the effort required for reading would restrict the second, less obvious dimension of meaning to a select circle of likeminded individuals. Actual propaganda— Hitler leaves no room for doubt on this score—does not play out in the medium of writing but in declamatory agitation. Only an orator can instantly gauge the public's reaction and adjust what he says accordingly, "until at length even the last group of an opposition, by its very bearing and facial expression, enables him to recognize its capitulation to his arguments"; only through speech, not written instruction, can the "resistance of emotions" be overcome.[42]

On their own, these observations are not very original. Hitler hones them to make a point of significant import, however, when he declares that the effects of declamatory agitation provide the sole measure of their "truth." An extended passage on the matter is revealing:

All propaganda must be popular and its intellectual level must be adjusted to the most limited intelligence among those it is addressed to. Consequently, the greater the mass it is intended to reach, the lower its purely intellectual level will have to be. ... The more modest its intellectual ballast, the more exclusively it takes into consideration the emotions of the masses, the more effective it will be. And this is the best proof of the soundness or unsoundness of a propaganda campaign, and not success in pleasing a few scholars or young aesthetes.[43]

Verification of the facts, nuance, decorum, and "criteria of humanitarianism and beauty"[44]—in other words, all the guiding values of cultivated, bourgeois-academic discourse—are deemed irrelevant, consigned to a self-satisfied world apart, and subjected to ridicule. This anti-academic tone, which hands the "scientifically trained intelligentsia"[45] over to open contempt, has nothing original about it, either. Hitler shares this view with a host of populist sectarians at the turn of the century, from whose writings he drew—parties who had forged an autodidactic and megalomaniacal counterworld to the sphere of professional academics. The credo of these "theoreticians of race and explainers of the world"[46] held that conventional scientific or scholarly accuracy does not matter. With that, they made the intellectual edifice they tinkered together impervious to objections from academic experts. Moreover, the same means that sectarians use to seal themselves off into elitist circles can be struck into populist coin, provided it achieves resonance. Ultimately, it serves a large-scale political ideology that need not worry about being proven wrong so long as it continues to produce desired effects. When the "accuracy or inaccuracy of propaganda" is measured only in terms of "success," it closes itself off into a tautological circle of self-verification: it garners belief because it presents itself as the truth, and it counts as true because the masses believe in it.

Here, a factor enters the equation that is consistently underestimated by those who view only error, blindness, or illusion at work in demagoguery—and, accordingly, seek to oppose it by means of reasonable objections. Counter to what such enlightened optimists believe, the demagogue—along with those in his train—usually knows full well what he is doing. He does not advance his claims *in spite of* the fact that they will offend reasonable people but *because* he can be sure to provoke them by doing so. The reflexive outrage he triggers does not unsettle him; rather, it affords him a kind of contemptuous exhilaration. In *Mein Kampf*, Hitler openly declares that propaganda is a means to an end. It is supposed to make "everyone ... convinced that the fact is real";[47] therefore, it excludes debate of the matter's merit—or lack thereof. Propaganda's "very first precondition," according to Hitler, is a "basically subjective and one-sided attitude ... toward every question it deals with."[48] Even though his rhetoric does not discount the truth as a category of appeal,[49] in the broader context of everything else he writes, it represents a secondary consideration deriving from the power of speech itself—that is, something constituted in circular fashion by the efficacy and force of pure assertion.[50]

When Hitler discusses the propagandistic fabrication of truth in the process of declamation, he elaborates a circular logic, too. The agitator, as described in *Mein Kampf*, entertains a direct connection to the feelings of the crowd that he is haranguing, and he seeks to absorb each and every swell of emotion. It is easy to picture how, during his early years in Munich, the author tested the guiding principles of his worldview for their rhetorical efficacy—until they finally seemed to be what the people actually believed. At the same time, Hitler stresses the need "to take a position in important questions of principle against all public opinion when it [assumes] a false attitude—disregarding all consideration of popularity, hatred, or struggle." In other words, the Party is not allowed to subordinate itself to public opinion; it must command it. Here and elsewhere, Hitler formulates the matter in sexualized terms: "It must not become a servant of the masses but their master!"[51] The point is not to subdue the audience by force, then, but to employ an imperious folksiness [*Volkstümlichkeit*] that is commensurate with the "feminine" disposition of the people[52]—which must also be protected from "seducers" on the enemy side.

6

Through his statements about the collective nature of the masses (feminine, with little "capacity for understanding," and notoriously forgetful),[53] Hitler draws the more select part of his readership—that is, those who read past early chapters (which are more anecdotal and autobiographical)[54]—into an exclusive compact among men who belong to a political avant-garde. But that is not the only—or even the most important—reward he distributes among initiates. He offers still more—the thrill of stepping behind the scenes of political power and now, with an insider's privileges, witnessing the process whereby an ideology is creatively constituted.

Mein Kampf does not afford this prospect with an ironic wink or the cynical grin attending lies that the author himself does not believe. Instead, it occurs with the grim determination of a decisionist. It is all a matter of the resolve with which one champions one's beliefs—and this bearing makes belief itself into a matter of decision. Showing oneself to be steadfast and unwavering has two sides—one that deters and another that initiates. Hitler knew well that his radicalism—separating the wheat from the chaff, in his view—had a polarizing effect, and this factored into his calculations.[55] All the same, it did not mean that his core adherents were loyal to their leader out of conviction alone. If anything, adherents' reasons for following amounted to molded clay resting on an underlying, organizational structure that was held in place by varying degrees of willingness to show and embody resolve.[56] Firmness of resolve—not blind obedience to ideology—constituted the primal matter connecting National Socialist actors. This unity was sufficiently strong and appealing to counterbalance centrifugal tendencies in a system that otherwise was dominated by rivalry and competition for rank. It was even compatible with silent scorn for the *Führer*. As research has shown, young planning experts in the National Socialist state demonstrated an "aloofly condescending relationship to Hitler, whom they certainly esteemed as a mass agitator and organizer, but did not give high marks for political thinking."[57] Such disdain did not harm the National Socialist system, however. On the contrary, the self-termed "spiritual" elite [*die Elite der "Geistigen"*] of radical, right-wing intellectuals recognized the opportunity to put its own stamp on the National Socialist movement, "given [its] weak ideological and theoretical profile."[58] Such parties could delude themselves that they were using the *Führer* politically and had trumped him ideologically.[59]

Here, in silhouette, it becomes clear how the deficiencies in Hitler's overwrought broadsheet contributed to the historical success of National Socialism. The "heterogeneous conglomeration" constituting the Nazi worldview managed "to give many things to many people—to satisfy the most varied instincts, needs, imaginings, and longings." Viewed from this angle, it was not the stark clarity of pronouncements so much as the indeterminacy of the program that paved the way for the NSDAP's rise from a small, sectarian group to a political party that enjoyed majority support.[60] If National Socialist ideology operated with polemical catchphrases that were largely devoid of meaning, it appealed, by this very fact, to groups that sought to fill the empty words with intellectual content of their own devising.[61]

Emptiness and resolve do not stand in contradiction; they complement and complete each other. As much may be gathered from Hitler's polemic, provided that one pays attention less to the statements that it makes than to the specific way that it uses language. *Mein Kampf* also operates on another level—offering instruction and inducements without requiring that one believe Hitler's every word. Hitler did not invite his inner circle to share in blind fanaticism so much as to enjoy language that wields force—performative empowerment on both rhetorical and political registers that used conventional modes of legitimation insofar as they were available but derived its hiddenmost and deepest joy in the fortified groundlessness of its own speech.

7

Evidence abounds that an anti-Semitic bearing is compatible with avowed decisionism. The Vienna mayor Karl Lueger—Hitler's foremost model in terms of populist animosity toward Jews—is said to have declared, "I decide who's a Jew!"[62] This may have been a matter of unabashed political opportunism—as was often alleged of Lueger. However, related statements also occur at the heart of National Socialist professions of faith. In *Michael*, his autobiographically inspired novel of political awakening, Joseph Goebbels reconciles the "Christ-Socialism" that he originally advocated with the anti-Semitism that he subsequently took over from Hitler:

> Christ cannot have been a Jew. I do not need to prove this with science or scholarship. It is so![63]
>
> Christ is the genius of love, as such the most diametrical opposite of Judaism, which is the incarnation of hate. The Jew is a non-race among the races of the earth. ... Christ is the first great enemy of the Jews. ... That is why Judaism had to get rid of him. For he was shaking the very foundations of its future international power.
>
> ...

Christ Socialists: That means voluntarily and willingly doing what the run-of-the-mill socialists do out of pity or for reasons of state.

Moral necessity versus political insight.

The struggle we are waging today until victory or the bitter end is, in its deepest sense, a struggle between Christ and Marx.

Christ: the principle of love.

Marx: the principle of hate.[64]

The novel depicts a man returning from war who is unable to reintegrate himself into civilian life and awaits the dawning of a new political and religious day. As in Hitler's account of his life, academic failure becomes part of a self-image that no longer pays heed to objections voiced by scholars and scientists.[65] Instead—and pithily, in his own fashion—Goebbels stresses empty readiness to believe as the character trait defining the war generation: "Youth today is more alive than ever before. Youth believes. In what? That is the gist of the struggle."[66] This will to believe, without aim as yet, is the vessel into which Hitler—coded in the novel as a nameless, charismatic orator[67]—would pour his ideological decisionism.[68]

The force of decision does not rest just on linguistic positing, however. Propagandistic words of power would remain largely without effect if they were not embedded in organized violence. Delivering a successful speech in the beer hall involved not just rhetorical attunement but also a security force that added emphasis by throwing out opponents or beating them up.[69] Although, as Hitler recognized, "brutal force" without a *Weltanschauung* behind it proves ineffective in the long term,[70] agitation derives its effect from accompanying terror, which suppresses any and all contradiction. Violence and ideology reinforce each other.

Mein Kampf also admits different readings with respect to such reciprocal reinforcement. The book's tenor hardly seems different from Hitler's public declamations. One might be tempted to conclude that it is addressed to the same audience—the "people." However, *Mein Kampf* is not directly aimed at crowds that are attending strictly organized party assemblies (and brawls) and are looking for communal experience and the "home" of a worldview. Indeed, such people make an appearance in the book only in the third-person plural, as the objects of propaganda. Instead, Hitler discusses strategies for staging events and provides detailed instructions intended for specialized use. Yet even this does not constitute the appeal of the chapters in question. Rather, their appeal derives from an unabashedly triumphant sentiment at how others—the Reds, the bourgeoisie—may be brought to heel by the ruthless use of force. By Hitler's account, the *we* group incorporates everyone who feels uplifted by seeing enemies beaten bloody in order to put a halt to disagreement once and for all. The "kick" that *Mein Kampf* offers to cooler and calmer readers does not concern a specific conviction wrested from competing opinions but the absolute refusal to engage in dialogue. It is wholly immaterial, then, whether one inwardly believes what Hitler says in his rants. It is even possible—as was the case for some of the more intellectual figures in

Nazi elites—to make fun of his pseudoscientific racial doctrine, to cover one's mouth and smirk at his forced speaking style, but still to experience the reflexive impulse to persecute any disrespectful comment made by third parties. A menacing vacuum emanates from *Mein Kampf*—a license for adherents to react to opposition with a "Just you wait" that bristles with lustful sadism. Such power to reinforce group belonging functions on an entirely different level than ideological obedience in the narrower sense. In the spectrum of signals that Hitler's book broadcasts, the inner circle of the National Socialist movement tuned in at this frequency.

To many onlookers, Hitler cut a comical figure. He shares this trait with other dictators who, notwithstanding the terror they spread, somehow seem ludicrous. The cabaret artist Serdar Somuncu, who performed readings from *Mein Kampf* in the 1990s, put it this way: "Hitler plus power is gruesome, but Hitler minus power is a comedy."[71] It might follow, then, that terror provides a necessary means for self-declared political leaders, trying to compensate for their lack of legitimate power through megalomania, to conceal their secret ridiculousness from followers and victims alike. If one examines *Mein Kampf* in terms of the ingredients that are used to cook up the worldview offered, then Hitler was just one of many self-taught crackpots hawking homebrewed intellectual concoctions during the crisis-ridden decades following the turn of the century. What was said at the very outset of this essay applies to his person, too: radical political movements feed on an intellectual precariat of bohemians and academic dropouts, throwing together various elements that they have found in the neurotic overproduction of private mythologies.

That said, it is not enough to view terror only as a defense against unintentionally comic effects—to reduce its function to intimidating the people who stand laughing at the sidelines. Nor do comic effects occur only when one manages to look away from actual terror. Disconcertingly, they adhere to terror itself—to the most horrible and real things that human beings can inflict on other human beings. It has been remarked time and again that cruelty borders on comedy inasmuch as it, too, proves incomprehensible. If one fails to find a meaningful context for one's suffering— however difficult it may still be to comprehend—then even the most brutal deeds can seem wholly unreal. Terrorist regimes have the common trait of sealing themselves off from outside, into self-contained purposefulness that is both opaque and absurd; in consequence, they stand uncannily close to comedy, where all meaning implodes.

But the sense that comedy and naked violence have an affinity is not just passive in nature. Those who wield power acknowledge the same feeling in their triumphalism—and this fact represents an important component of the psychology of perpetrators. Under the right circumstances, arbitrary acts of self-satisfied omnipotence, which refuse any explanation to their victims, may occasion fits of laughter. Ernst Jünger's description of one such moment offers insights into the fascist sensibility. "In March of 1921," he writes in his 1934 essay, *On Pain*,

I witnessed the clash of a three-person machine-gun squad with a demonstration march comprised of as many as 5,000 participants. A minute after the order to fire was given, the demonstrators vanished from the scene even though not one single person had been injured. The sight of this event had something magical about it; it evoked that deep sense of delight which takes hold of one when an ignoble demon is unmasked. At any rate, participation in repelling such an unfounded claim to authority is more instructive than the lessons learned from an entire library of sociological studies.[72]

Standing before a commando of the Reichswehr, the demonstrators' "claim to authority" is "unfounded" inasmuch as their demands can take the form of only an appeal. But the paramilitary squad's threat of violence is "unfounded," too—as were, not too long afterward, interventions by security forces and Sturmabteilung (SA) (Storm Trooper) toughs whose "ruthless energy" and "brutal activism" delighted Hitler.[73] Jünger's cheery mood has nothing to do with contentment at the greater legitimacy of his side's actions; it stems from satisfaction that all efforts to arrive at understanding have abruptly been put to an end. Staring into the muzzle of a gun, it is meaningless to claim to know better—unless one wants to risk the manifest ridiculousness that, from a sufficiently detached standpoint, attaches to all instances of impotent outrage. Conversely, the party with weapons on his side need not waste words, see things from his opponent's viewpoint, negotiate, or even try to persuade anybody.

It is not just the contrast between one's own executive power and the powerlessness of the opposition that incites laughter but also the freedom to lift oneself above the other's claim to communicative meaning of any sort. Providing adherents with sense and ideological justification represents only the outermost sphere of activity in totalitarian movements. The center is occupied by elites that, in Hannah Arendt's words, need no proofs and

> are not even supposed to believe in the literal truth of ideological clichés. These are fabricated to answer a quest for truth among the masses which in its insistence on explanation still has much in common with the normal world. The elite is not composed of ideologists; its members' whole education is aimed at abolishing their capacity for distinguishing between truth and falsehood, between reality and fiction. Their superiority consists in their capacity immediately to dissolve every statement of fact into a declaration of purpose.[74]

8

None of the reflections offered here is meant to discount the fact that Hitler's *Mein Kampf* stands as an ideological pamphlet of the most extreme kind. Not only does the chapter "Nation and Race" contain the entire arsenal of rabble-rousing against Jews, it also lays out the program for their elimination. Because Hitler ties his hatred for Jews closely to the battlefront against Marxism and situates these core fields of his program in a panorama of world-historical dimensions, one is left with the impression that he is presenting a closed structure of thought with full conviction. However, this is not the sole message of the book—nor, for readers of a cooler constitution, was it necessarily the most important. In addition to the propagandistic asseverations, a second signal is being broadcasted—one that would have appealed to the "innermost stratum of the totalitarian hierarchy" that, in Arendt's words, is distinguished by "freedom from the content of its own ideology."[75] The young jurists, social engineers, and large-scale planners who came to operate the levers of power in the National Socialist system did not number among the enthusiastic readers of *Mein Kampf*, just as they had no time for the ham-fisted anti-Semitism of run-of-the-mill Nazis. All the same, the framework of the program that Hitler designed afforded them latitude for radical visions of their own—with the consequence that the National Socialist system facilitated rapid professional advancement. For this group, National Socialism was a tool, not a religion.[76]

Mein Kampf presents such a perspective insofar as it offers its readership a broad array of potential gratifications. To a nation traumatized by war and defeat, it promises to restore lost honor and the means to achieve new greatness; it gives wayward individuals a sense of direction; it turns ambivalence into clear-cut meaning to be worked out with unbridled hatred. All of this amounts to satisfying the wish for a coherent, "fictitious world"[77]—as reflected by Hitler's vision of a state order founded on racial biology. All the while (on a harmonic register, as it were), *Mein Kampf* communicates another desire (and pleasure) too, one that savors the power of empty words that make an impact—the fascination of power deriving strictly from its own ascent, which fashions itself out of nothing. This proximity to the void has been interpreted as nihilism and attributed to philosophical influences. Ultimately, however, it derives from a way of using language rather than from a system of ideas— a use of language that does not articulate and lend form to anything preexisting but takes joy, simply in the pure power of its manifestation, by commanding being and nothingness, life and death.[78]

III

PROSPECTS AND CONSEQUENCES

Following the catastrophe of the Second World War and the Holocaust, political elites became convinced that Europe would experience a new political beginning only by overcoming the curse of destructive nationalism. The European balance of peace should have a democratic, liberal, and, above all, postnational shape. Accordingly, the project of European unification also harbored the idea of a collective learning process.

So long as the continent—notwithstanding its waning influence in terms of world politics—continued to enjoy a privileged global position and so long as efforts at political integration offered a credible prospect for the increased prosperity of all, this European "learning community" aimed for considerable advances. However, since the 1990s, conditions favoring such endeavors have no longer consistently prevailed. Economic competition on a global scale, radical movements, wars at its borders, and, most recently, the influx of refugees have placed Europe—which has remained stuck halfway between a federation of states and a supragovernmental formation—under immense pressure. While the push for coordination between European institutions across borders proceeds, it is impossible not to see that, in the various national public spheres (which remain as important as ever), the "European idea" is weakening. The corollary is louder and louder chauvinism. At its core, it retains the xenophobia of old, even if racial markers of foreignness have largely been replaced by religious and cultural ones. Likewise, anti-Semitism has been crawling out from the marginal spaces, having long been taboo in the public sphere. The political landscape is becoming polarized in a way that recalls the interwar period (even if this does not mean that a new era of totalitarianism is imminent). Populist movements are gaining in strength everywhere. Meanwhile, some countries are already being restructured constitutionally—away from democracy and the rule of law, toward authoritarianism. None of this is possible without rousing the specters of nationalism that seemed to have been buried under the ruins in 1945—nor can it fail to reactivate the political-journalistic cadre described in the first part of this essay. At rallies and on Internet forums—indeed, in party leadership—firebrands are staking claims, however far-fetched, to fuel conflict and escalate matters beyond the sphere of civil debate.

All of this raises the question of how comprehensive and enduring the learning process that occurred after the Second World War really was. Indeed, there are good reasons to believe that human beings never learn from history for long. Each generation comes up with its own way of seeing the world, and this perspective has limited room for the experiences of the generations preceding it. For this reason alone, a straightforward learning process cannot be expected. It seems that whenever certain situations of conflict emerge, corresponding sociocultural patterns of reaction will persistently recur. Such reactions depend far more on the acuteness of present conditions than on cumulative knowledge derived from the past. This is especially true when political actors seek to mint political capital from the temporary power they hold. From this angle, history amounts to repetition with variation, and it runs counter to the Enlightenment hope that humankind, as a collective, can learn from past catastrophes and make fitting adjustments to its practices of communal life.

But all the same, historical precedents do admit conclusions that may influence practical action. A retrospective examination of National Socialism can shed some light on the dynamic of fanaticization. In conclusion, then, three points merit emphasis.

1. Fanaticism is not blind. This qualification applies only to the most clueless and insignificant members of a movement. At the top, among architects and leaders, fanaticism represents an item of reflection that proves all but hysterical. Its modes of expression and the reactions of others—condescension, indignation, horror, and so on—are matters of wary and precise calculation. The system always assigns, in advance, a role to those who would seek to counter it with superior insight: their part is to endure abuse and opprobrium. Because fanaticism limits options for speech by acknowledging a tightly restricted sphere of truth—beyond which the enemy terrain of deviant opinion already begins—it has no room for dialogue. Indeed, because discussion would undermine his position, the fanatic views it as the mode in which only the weak communicate. But at the same time—and precisely because he scornfully refuses dialogue—the fanatic is constantly and obsessively drawn to his avowed enemy. This holds even when the putative enemy has been eliminated. Fanaticism would lose its core, driving

force without paranoid clairvoyance that spills over into the purely fantastic.

2. Fanaticization does not necessarily arise from genuine conviction. As the example of Hitler illustrates, its beginnings often lie in a chance identification, in relative terms, of the options afforded by the market of opinion. In this stage, the primary concern is to become the spokesman for what has been neglected until now or pursued only halfheartedly. From this position, competency in a specific area and advocacy for a *we* group may be claimed.

One's relative situation in the field of possible utterances determines the actual contents with which this position is then filled. Generally, middle registers of opinion are more densely populated than marginal ones. Thus, by making extreme pronouncements, a speaker can establish a stronger rhetorical position for himself. The form that such declarations assume depends on the resonance that earlier pronouncements meet with. Often, the speaker will move toward the middle ground by making concessions and toning down his message; in this way, he is able to secure political alliances. But in periods of sustained social tension, such an approach does not promise the greatest success. Then, driven by encouragement from parties that he himself has indoctrinated, the speaker will test out the viability of further radicalization. Hereby, radicalism and strategy, fanaticism and political opportunism, work in concert. As a matter of calculation, even drifting off into seeming absurdity may prove advisable insofar as the "base" puts a premium on flights of enthusiasm, which signal initiation to insiders and confirm that the consensus of others does not matter. A contributing factor warranting mention is the fact that, as a rule, marginal groups think they are not adequately represented in the sphere of prevailing social rationality. Accordingly, they reach for forms of expression that count as largely irrational in the eyes of majoritarian society.

The primary objective of ideological pronouncements is *power of authority*. First and foremost, it is the spokesman himself who gains power, solidifies his claim to leadership in a certain sector of political opinion, and defends his role against competitors. But to recruit followers, he must offer chances to participate. This occurs on many levels—by describing social ills in a way that appeals to the target audience's needs and instincts, by making it desirable to join in the hunt for those who have caused them, and by offering the prospect of rising from insignificance and becoming a member of a community that is in the process of constituting itself in full self-awareness. Still, the greatest promise the spokesman makes is the power of authority itself. The language involved naturally veers toward excess. The secret to its success lies, not least of all, in its own self-intoxication. Anyone who adopts this language comes to share in its transports. This is the "Dionysian" component of fanatical movements.

This autocatalytic effect is one of the reasons that the leader need not *believe* all that he says. Nor does his audience have to, either. All that is necessary is for both sides to come to an understanding that they will base their

community on ostentatious adherence to extreme pronouncements, embrace the transports of self-intoxication,
and trouble outsiders with their triumphal displays. Half-
truths prove especially suited to this kind of pact because
they offer greater flexibility, appear more credible to anyone
who is still wavering, and, finally, are difficult to refute. That
said, when the leader and his followers are on the same
page, flat-out lies prove effective, too. By repeating and ritu-
ally solidifying lies, those who tell and hear them may, after
a while, embrace them as articles of faith—even though
doing so is not necessary from the inception. A general
human predisposition exists to credit one's own lies, even
when one knows they are just that. This may be explained,
on the one hand, by the tendency to avoid cognitive disso-
nance by fitting perceptions to one's overall bearing, thereby
lessening the expenditure of psychic energy. On the other
hand, lies that prove effective represent a semantic investment that can be abandoned only at a high price. As soon as
a falsehood has become part of a group identity, it gener-
ates new obligations—which can be neglected only at risk
of showing weakness or, worse still, a treasonous attitude.
Time and again, the historical record has shown how the
incendiaries of radical movements are taken prisoner by
their own words, as it were. As confrontations mount—and
along with them, group pressure—they have no choice but
to earnestly embrace what might have started out as a
game with rhetorical fire and could have gone up in smoke.
When this occurs, fanaticism consumes its "creator."

3. Fanatical movements are not uniform, and they bundle together motivations that are exceedingly varied—even though this circumstance contradicts the image that they try to project. By annexing, as it were, a problematic sphere that is important to many people, they maintain a connection to the world beyond, their hermetic mode of organization notwithstanding. At the same time, their strategy does not concern the factual elimination of economic or political ills so much as mobilizing emotions that play a key role when unfavorable conditions prevail—feelings of injustice, humiliation, and dishonor. Even the actions of terrorist organizations must be understood in light of this embittered idealism. Violence, the seemingly arbitrary way victims are chosen, and even excessively cruel practices are intended as justified reactions to the injustice that long-suffering radicals have made their fundamental cause. Moreover, committing horrific deeds together forges a conspiratorial coherence that ensures the loyalty of new arrivals. Likewise, the movement casts a spell, particularly on male recruits, with its—often markedly ascetic—internal discipline and readiness to perform violence against outsiders. In this way, as members pursue their own interests, the core ideological concern accommodates an array of secondary motivations that often connect to it only loosely—attention getting, the thrill of adventure, compensation for personal setbacks, the exalted sensation of taking the field for something important, the pleasure of burdening the enemy with all the guilt, submissive yearnings, and, last but not least—and in uncanny proximity to this love of discipline—the allure of letting go and cutting loose.

It would be mistaken to assign all of this to the powerful influence of a doctrine or declare it a matter of mass delusion. Analysis must begin elsewhere—that is, with the *opportunities* that radicalization creates. Among all the options and meanings that life affords, there are extremely varied reasons—which only rarely prove purely ideological in nature—why a sizeable number of human beings would *decide* to make such a program their own.

Notes

PART I

1. On the distinction between "cold" and "hot" sign systems, see Albrecht Koschorke, *Wahrheit und Erfindung. Grundzüge einer Allgemeinen Erzähltheorie* (Frankfurt a.M.: Fischer, 2012), 12 ff.

2. Gustave Le Bon, *The Crowd: A Study of the Popular Mind* (New York: Macmillan, 1897), 113.

3. "There is, thus, a simple answer to the question of why the masses do not revolt—a perennial problem for social stratification—and it does not concern value consensus, or force, or exchange in the usual sense of those conventional sociological explanations. The masses comply because they lack collective organization to do otherwise, because they are embedded within collective and distributive power organizations controlled by others. They are *organizationally outflanked*." Michael Mann, *The Sources of Social Power*, vol. 1, *A History of Power from the Beginning to A.D. 1760* (Cambridge: Cambridge University Press, 2012), 7.

4. Le Bon, *The Crowd*, 126.

5. Cf. Rolf Reichardt, "Die Stiftung von Frankreichs nationaler Identität durch die Selbstmystifizierung der Französischen Revolution am Beispiel der 'Bastille,'" in *Mythos und Nation. Studien zur Entwicklung des kollektiven Bewußtseins in der Neuzeit*, vol. 3, ed. Helmut Berding (Frankfurt a.M.: Suhrkamp, 1996), 133–163. Reichardt points out that the motto *Liberté, egalité, fraternité*, now associated with the French Revolution—not least of all because it stands emblazoned at the entryway of every French town hall—was not in

wide use during revolutionary times. It was first popularized by "the republican movement of the nineteenth century, largely animated by secular schoolteachers and socialists" (136).

6. Robert Darnton, *The Literary Underground of the Old Regime* (Cambridge, MA: Harvard University Press, 1982), 20.

7. Ibid., 17.

8. Ibid., 19.

9. Ibid., 40.

10. "German women and a German's word, / German wine and German song, / May they keep, the world o'er, / Their dulcet ring, had so long" ("Deutsche Frauen, deutsche Treue, / Deutscher Wein und deutscher Sang / Sollen in der Welt behalten / Ihren alten schönen Klang"). August Heinrich Hoffmann von Fallersleben, "Lied der Deutschen," 1841.

11. Hans-Martin Blitz, *Aus Liebe zum Vaterland. Die deutsche Nation im 18. Jahrhundert* (Hamburg: Hamburger Edition, 2000), 217.

12. Eric J. Hobsbawm, *Nations and Nationalism since 1780: Programme Myth, Reality* (Cambridge: Cambridge University Press, 1990), 104.

13. Ulrich Bielefeld, *Nation und Gesellschaft. Selbstthematisierungen in Frankreich und Deutschland* (Hamburg: Hamburger Edition, 2003), 14.

14. Ibid., 15.

15. Joseph Goebbels, *Michael*, trans. Joachim Neugroschel (New York: Amok, 1987), 14.

16. Jacques Sémelin, *Purify and Destroy: The Political Uses of Massacre and Genocide*, trans. Cynthia Schoch (New York: Columbia University Press, 2007), 55.

17. Ibid., 61.

18. For individual case studies—Benito Mussolini, Josef Stalin, Kim Il-Sung, Mao Zedong, Muammar Gaddafi, Saddam Hussein, and others—in light of their literary borrowings, see Albrecht Koschorke and Konstantin Kaminskij, eds., *Despoten dichten. Sprachkunst und Gewalt* (Konstanz: Konstanz University Press, 2011).

19. A fuller discussion occurs in the introduction to Koschorke and Kaminskij, *Despoten dichten*, 9–26, here 17–21. Cf. the classic study by Hannah Arendt, *The Origins of Totalitarianism* (New York: Harcourt, 1994).

20. Le Bon, *The Crowd*, 113.

21. Quoted in Barbara Babcock, "'The Arts and All Things Common': Victor Turner's Literary Anthropology," *Comparative Criticism* 9 (1987): 39–46, here 42.

22. Laurent Bazin, "Der Geist eines neuen Nationalismus. Was Elfenbeinküste und Usbekistan gemeinsam haben," *Le Monde diplomatique*, German edition, March 2010, 6.

23. Cf. Riccardo Nicolosi, "Saparmyrat Nyýazows Ruhnama und die Erfindung Turkmenistans," in Koschorke and Kaminskij, *Despoten dichten*, 301–323. Arto Halonen has made an insightful documentary film about Saparmurat Niyazov's book *Ruhnama, or Book of the Soul*, called *Shadow of the Holy Book* (2007).

24. For an example, see the introduction by Adolf Stern to Theodor Körner, *Werke: Erster Teil* (Stuttgart: Union Deutsche Verlagsgesellschaft, 1889), i–xxxii.

PART II

1. Albrecht Koschorke and Konstantin Kaminskij, eds., *Despoten dichten. Sprachkunst und Gewalt* (Konstanz: Konstanz University Press, 2011).

2. Cf. Riccardo Nicolosi, "Saparmyrat Nyýazows Ruhnama und die Erfindung Turkmenistans," in Koschorke and Kaminskij, *Despoten dichten*.

3. This is the tenor of researchers who are working on the new edition put out by the Munich Institute for Contemporary History. Cf. the interview conducted by *Die Zeit*, accessible online at http://www.zeit.de/2013/40 hitler-mein-kampf-kritische-edition-ifz-bayern. Even this reprinting, accompanied by countless source-critical notes, is being handled as a hot potato by the book trade. Cf. the articles in *Der Spiegel*, online at www.spiegel.de/kultur/gesellschaft/mein-kampf-kann-man-hitlers-hetzschrift-jetzt-einfach-kaufen-a-1068642.html and www.spiegel.de/kultur/gesellschaft/mein-kampf-in-kritischer-editionauf3700-fussnoten-gegen-adolf-hitlers-hass-a-1068562.html.

4. See Othmar Plöckinger, *Geschichte eines Buches: Adolf Hitlers "Mein Kampf" 1922–1945* (Munich: Oldenbourg, 2006), 225ff., for a list of such assessments up to 1933.

5. For the fullest inventory, cf. ibid.

6. Adolf Hitler, *Mein Kampf*, trans. Ralph Manheim (Boston: Houghton Mifflin, 1998), 37ff.

7. Ibid., 42, translation modified.

8. Ibid., 43–44.

9. Ibid., 44.

10. Philippe Lejeune, *Le pacte autobiographique: Signes de vie* (Paris: Seuil, 2005).

11. Brigitte Hamann, *Hitler's Vienna: A Dictator's Apprenticeship*, trans. Thomas Thornton (New York: Oxford University Press, 1999), 142–143. This account differs from the reconstruction of Hitler's Vienna period in Werner Maser, *Adolf Hitler Mein Kampf. Geschichte, Auszüge, Kommentare* (Esslingen: Bechtle, 1981).

12. Hamann, *Hitler's Vienna*, 141ff.

13. Hitler, *Mein Kampf*, 21.

14. Ibid., 30.

15. Ibid., 42.

16. Cf. Barbara Zehnpfennig, *Hitlers Mein Kampf. Eine Interpretation* (Munich: Fink, 2000), 76f.

17. Hannah Arendt, *The Origins of Totalitarianism* (New York: Harcourt, 1994), 357.

18. This comes out most clearly in a later passage concerning the end of the First World War: "The more I occupied myself with the idea of a necessary change in the government's attitude toward Social Democracy as the momentary embodiment of Marxism, the more I recognized the lack of a serviceable substitute for this doctrine. What would be given the masses, if, just supposing, Social Democracy had been broken? There was not one movement in existence, which could have been expected to succeed in drawing into its sphere of influence the great multitudes of workers grown more or less leaderless." Hitler, *Mein Kampf*, 173.

19. Cf. Hamann, *Hitler's Vienna*, 252.

20. In the chapter entitled "Significance of the Spoken Word," Hitler writes that it is advisable "always to raise the possible objections oneself, immediately, and prove their untenability; in this way the listener, even stuffed full of half-taught objections but otherwise possessed of an honest heart, is won over more easily through the preemptive removal of the doubts that have been impressed on his mind. The half-learned stuff is automatically overturned and one's attention more and more attracted by the presentation." *Mein Kampf*, 523.

21. Ibid., 51ff.

22. Ibid., 56.

23. Ibid., 51.

24. On this "love contract" that dictators seal with the people, see Albrecht Koschorke, "Taten aus Worten. Über den fiktiven Kern von Gewaltherrschaft," in *Dichter und Lenker. Die Literatur der Staatsmänner, Päpste und Despoten von der Frühen Neuzeit bis in die Gegenwart*, ed. Patrick Ramponi and Saskia Wiedner (Tübingen: Francke, 2014), 33–48.

25. Hitler, *Mein Kampf*, 202.

26. Ibid.

27. Ibid.

28. Ibid., 206.

29. Ibid.

30. On the book's diffusion, see the details provided by Plöck-inger, *Geschichte eines Buches*, 424ff., as well as Christian Alexander Braun and Christiane Friederike Marxhausen, "Adolf Hitlers *Mein Kampf*. Herrschaftssymbol, Herrschaft-sinstrument, Medium ideologischer Kommunikation," in Koschorke and Kaminskij, *Despoten dichten*, 179–209.

31. Hitler, *Mein Kampf*, vii.

32. Ibid., 470, 477–479.

33. Arendt, *Origins of Totalitarianism*, 376–378.

34. This is the tendency in most accounts. See, for example, the relevant passage in Joachim C. Fest, *Hitler*, trans. Richard Winston and Clara Winston (New York: Harcourt Brace Jovanovich, 1974), which details Hitler's views while offering abundant stylistic criticism. Fest describes Hitler's hatred of Jews as "a pathological mania" without discounting "the propaganda value of his anti-Semitism" (211).

35. Hamann, *Hitler's Vienna*, 352; cf. Ian Kershaw, *Hitler, 1889–1936: Hubris* (New York: Norton, 2000). Kershaw explains Hitler's account in terms of tactics. After the failed putsch, he had to fashion a certain image—the self-portrait "of the nobody who struggled from the first against adversity, and, rejected by the academic 'establishment,' taught himself through painstaking study, coming—above all through his own bitter experiences—to unique insights into politics and society that enabled him without assistance at around twenty to formulate a rounded 'world view.' This unchanged 'world view,' he was saying in 1924, provided him with the claim to the leadership of the national movement and indeed to be

Germany's coming 'great leader.' ... An admission that he had become an ideological antisemite only after the war, as he lay blinded from mustard gas in a hospital in Pasewalk and heard of Germany's defeat and the revolution, would certainly have sounded less heroic and would also have smacked of hysteria" (65).

36. Hitler, *Mein Kampf*, 206. According to Ludolf Herbst, *Hitlers Charisma. Die Erfindung eines deutschen Messias* (Frankfurt a.M.: Fischer, 2010), Hitler was branded with ideological fanaticism only after the war. Previously, he had been a relatively shy and apolitical person living at the lower rungs of society. No unequivocal proof for his "anti-Semitic or anti-Marxist 'worldview'" can be found before 1919 (99). On this basis, Herbst concludes that the entire depiction of the Vienna period in *Mein Kampf* amounts to a self-serving mythological fabrication. Moreover, he convincingly demonstrates that Hitler did not arrive at his *Weltanschauung* autodidactically but rather under the patronage of the Reichswehr (99ff.). This only confirms the importance of examining Hitler's text in terms of narrative strategy, not factual "substance."

37. Just how accurately Hitler assessed the mood of his future adherents—harboring humanitarian qualms that would yield to racist convictions—is attested by the autobiographical account provided by a female National Socialist from the early 1930s. Quoted in Claudia Koonz, *Mütter im Vaterland. Frauen im Dritten Reich* (Freiburg: Kore, 1991), 79.

38. Cf. Plöckinger, *Geschichte eines Buches*, 121ff.

39. "Clearly, the oratorical style of the book was introduced only later." Ibid., 72.

40. This debunks the legend of Hitler's inherent charisma. Cf. Herbst, *Hitlers Charisma*, 109, for an account of how Hitler was drafted for training as a political propagandist "in the framework of official duties."

41. "As the foundation for every instance of public speaking," a publication from 1935 declares, "it was and remains self-evident to use the bible of National Socialism: Adolf Hitler's *Mein Kampf.* Anyone who felt himself growing weak in the fight drew new strength and new courage from his political bible." Quoted in Braun and Marxhausen, "Adolf Hitlers *Mein Kampf*," 201.

42. Hitler, *Mein Kampf,* 471.

43. Ibid., 180.

44. Ibid., 178.

45. Ibid., 179.

46. Thus the title of a very instructive chapter in Hamann, *Hitler's Vienna,* 200–235.

47. Hitler, *Mein Kampf,* 180.

48. Ibid., 182.

49. The following passage is symptomatic: "It was absolutely wrong to discuss war guilt from the standpoint that Germany alone could not be held responsible for the outbreak of the catastrophe; it would have been correct to load every bit of the blame on the shoulders of the enemy, even if this had not really corresponded to the true facts, as it actually did." Hitler, *Mein Kampf,* 182.

50. A similar view is offered by Josef Kopperschmidt, "Darf einem zu Hitler auch nichts einfallen? Thematisch einleitende Bemerkungen," in *Hitler der Redner,* ed. Josef Kopperschmidt (Munich: Fink, 2003), 11–27, who describes "rhetorical power" as a "model case of power dependent on approbation [*Musterfall von zustimmungsabhängiger Macht*]" (13).

51. Hitler, *Mein Kampf,* 465.

52. Ibid., 183. On Hitler's sexual symbolism, see Kenneth Burke, "The Rhetoric of Hitler's Battle," in *The Philosophy of Literary Form: Studies in Symbolic Action* (New York: Vintage, 1941), 191–220.

53. Hitler, *Mein Kampf*, 183.

54. For evidence concerning the very different ways that the various parts of *Mein Kampf* were received, see Plöckinger, *Geschichte eines Buches*, 429ff.

55. For instance, the following remark: "The more radical and inflammatory my propaganda was, the more this frightened weaklings and hesitant characters and prevented them from penetrating the primary core of our organization." *Mein Kampf*, 586.

56. On the tautological component of will and its bearing on literary developments around 1900, see Ingo Stöckmann, *Der Wille zum Willen. Der Naturalismus und die Gründung der literarischen Moderne 1880–1900* (Berlin: de Gruyter, 2009).

57. Ulrich Herbert, *Best. Biographische Studien über Radikalismus, Weltanschauung und Vernunft, 1903–1989* (Bonn: Dietz, 1996), 107.

58. Ibid., 104.

59. Cf. Karl-Dietrich Bracher, "Voraussetzungen des nationalsozialistischen Aufstiegs," in *Die Nationalsozialistische Machtergreifung. Studien zur Errichtung des nationalsozialistischen Herrschaftssystems in Deutschland*, ed. Karl-Dietrich Bracher, Wolfgang Sauer, and Gerhard Schulz (Opladen: Westdeutscher Verlag, 1962), 1–27; Per Leo, *Der Wille zum Wesen. Weltanschauungskultur, charakterologisches Denken und Judenfeindschaft in Deutschland 1890–1940* (Berlin: Matthes & Seitz, 2013), 16ff. In very concrete terms, Lutz Raphael has demonstrated that the National Socialist worldview should be understood "as a politically controlled, but intellectually open field of opinion" inasmuch as its "compulsory dimension was limited to just a few conceptual wrappers [*Begriffshülsen*]." "Radikales Ordnungsdenken und die Organisation totalitärer Herrschaft: Weltanschauungseliten

und Humanwissenschaftler im NS-Regime," *Geschichte und Gesellschaft* 27.1 (2001): 5–40, here 28.

60. Bracher, "Voraussetzungen," 22f.

61. Likewise Raphael, "Radikales Ordnungsdenken," 28 ff.

62. Hamann, *Hitler's Vienna*, 290, translation modified.

63. Joseph Goebbels, *Michael*, trans. Joachim Neugroschel (New York: Amok, 1987), 45.

64. Ibid., 65–66.

65. In *Michael*, it is expressed as follows: "What am I studying? Everything and nothing. I am too lazy and I think I am too stupid to specialize in anything. I want to become a man! I want to have a profile. Personality! The road to the new German!" (7): "Intellect is a danger to the development of the character" (9).

66. Ibid., 3.

67. Ibid., 82–83, 123–124.

68. On decisionism and voluntarism as defining traits of the Nazi ideology, see the foundational study by Uwe Hebekus, *Ästhetische Ermächtigung. Zum politischen Ort der Literatur im Zeitraum der Klassischen Moderne* (Munich: Fink, 2009), esp. 393ff. On the significance of decisionism in the 1920s in general, see Christian Graf von Krockow, *Die Entscheidung. Eine Untersuchung über Ernst Jünger, Carl Schmitt, Martin Heidegger* (Frankfurt a.M.: Campus, 1990).

69. Hitler, *Mein Kampf*, 483ff., esp. 489ff.

70. Ibid., 172: "Any attempt to combat a philosophy with methods of violence will fail in the end, unless the fight takes the form of attack for a new spiritual attitude. Only in the struggle between two philosophies can the weapon of brutal force, persistently and ruthlessly applied, lead to a decision for the side it supports."

71. Quoted in Othmar Plöckinger, "Rhetorik, Propaganda und Masse in Hitlers *Mein Kampf*," in Kopperschmidt, *Hitler der Redner*, 115–141, here 139.

72. Ernst Jünger, *On Pain*, trans. David C. Durst (New York: Telos, 2008), 25. For a more in-depth analysis of this episode, see Albrecht Koschorke, "Der Traumatiker als Faschist. Ernst Jüngers Essay 'Über den Schmerz,'" in *Modernität und Trauma. Beiträge zum Zeitenbruch des Ersten Weltkrieges*, ed. Inka Mülder-Bach (Vienna: Parabasen, 2000), 211–227, here 220f. Several formulations from this essay occur in the following.

73. Hitler, *Mein Kampf*, 483.

74. Arendt, *Origins of Totalitarianism*, 384–385. The quotation continues: "In distinction to the mass membership which, for instance, needs some demonstration of the inferiority of the Jewish race before it can safely be asked to kill Jews, the elite formations understand that the statement, all Jews are inferior, means, all Jews should be killed."

75. Ibid., 387.

76. "The National Socialist ideology was no matter of faith for most of these young, career-oriented experts. It simply offered them the most room to act freely." Götz Aly and Susanne Heim, *Vordenker der Vernichtung. Auschwitz und die deutschen Pläne für eine neue europäische Ordnung* (Hamburg: Hoffmann und Campe, 1991), 288.

77. "What distinguishes the totalitarian leaders and dictators is ... the simple-minded purposefulness with which they choose those elements of existing ideologies which are best fitted to become the fundaments of another, entirely fictitious world. ... Their art consists in using, and at the same time transcending, the elements of reality, of verifiable experience. With such generalizations, totalitarian propaganda establishes a world fit to compete with the real one, whose main handicap is that it is not logical, consistent, and organized. The consistency of

the fiction and strictness of the organization make it possible for the generalization eventually to survive the explosion of more specific lies." Arendt, *Origins of Totalitarianism*, 361–362.

78. Cf. Hebekus, *Ästhetische Ermächtigung*, and "Der Wille zur Form. Politischer Ästhetizismus bei Georg Simmel, Ernst H. Kantorowicz – und Alfred Rosenberg," in Uwe Hebekus and Ingo Stöckmann, eds., *Die Souveränität der Literatur. Zum Totalitären der Klassischen Moderne 1900–1933* (Munich: Fink, 2008), 45–75.